The Battle of Bunker Hill

by Daniel Rosen

Table of Contents

Introduction 2
Chapter One
The First Battles. 4
Chapter Two
The Battle on the Hill 8
Chapter Three
Who Won? 14
Conclusion. 20
Glossary 22
Index. 23
Comprehension Check 24

Introduction ★ ★ ★

In 1775 the American colonists were angry with Great Britain. For more than a century, colonists had thought of themselves as loyal subjects of the British king. Certainly the British and the colonists had argued, but they were able to solve their problems. But in 1775, things had become very tense.

For more than 10 years, the colonists and the British had argued fiercely about taxes. The trouble started after the British won the French and Indian War in 1763. The British had won all of eastern North America. Afterward the British wanted the colonists to pay for the war as well as for their own defense. They did this by charging the colonists new taxes.

The Boston Tea Party showed how angry the colonists were about British taxes.

The colonists were not only angry about the taxes. They also felt that British tax laws should not apply to them because they had no vote on the laws. Quickly, the argument turned from taxes to government. The colonists were used to ruling themselves. King George III wanted to show the colonists that he was the boss.

Boston became the center of colonial protests against the British. Samuel Adams and other **Patriots** called King George III a **tyrant**. In 1770 British troops killed six people in a riot known as the Boston **Massacre**. In 1773 during the Boston Tea Party, Patriots threw British tea into the harbor. They were protesting a tax they viewed as unfair. King George III had seen enough. He thought what was happening in the colonies was a stark case of **rebellion**. It was time to get tough.

★ ★ ★ Chapter One ★ ★ ★

The First Battles

The British governor of Massachusetts in 1775 was General Thomas Gage. To stop the colonists' rebellion, Gage had orders to arrest two Patriot leaders, Sam Adams and John Hancock. When British spies had found out that Hancock and Adams were hiding in the village of Lexington near Boston, Gage decided to act. The spies also told Gage that the Patriot **militia**, a group of colonists ready to fight, was in nearby Concord. This group, called the **Minutemen**, had hidden guns and gunpowder there.

The Patriots also had spies. They learned of the British plans. On the night of April 18, 1775, Paul Revere and two other riders rode to Lexington and Concord. They woke up the Minutemen. They told them that the British were marching to Lexington and Concord. At dawn on the morning of April 19, 1775, the British reached Lexington. They found a small force of Minutemen waiting for them.

The Intolerable Acts

After the Boston Tea Party the British were quick to strike back at the citizens of Boston. A new series of laws were put in place. The new laws closed the port of Boston, and forced the colonists to house British soldiers in their homes. The new laws made the colonists even angrier. The colonists called them the Intolerable Acts.

The Minutemen were mostly farmers and business owners and not trained soldiers.

In His Own Words Paul Revere

The British captured Paul Revere, but not before he had warned the Minutemen. Here he tells what happened:

"In an instant I saw four of them, who rode up to me with pistols [and] said, 'Stop. If you go an inch further, you are a dead man.'"

No one knows who fired the first shot. But when the smoke cleared, Minutemen lay dead. The British marched on to Concord where another group of Minutemen fought them. The British did not find Adams and Hancock, who had escaped. They also did not find the guns and gunpowder, which had been moved to a new hiding spot.

On the march back to Boston, Minutemen fired at the British from behind trees and stone walls. They killed nearly 100 British soldiers. The battles of Lexington and Concord marked the opening of the American Revolution. The British army was the strongest fighting force in the world. But the Patriots had shown that they were ready to fight for independence.

Patriot Spies

The British were shocked at the damage done by the Minutemen. But they felt the colonists did not fight "fair." Professional armies fought battles in the open. They did not fight from behind trees and rocks.

The British decided they needed to make their position in Boston stronger. There were two hills directly across the Charles River from Boston on the Charlestown peninsula. Breed's Hill was about 75 feet high. Bunker Hill was about 110 feet high. The British decided to send troops up the hills to keep the Patriots from getting them. General William Howe was the British commander. He decided he would teach "these upstart colonials" how real soldiers fought.

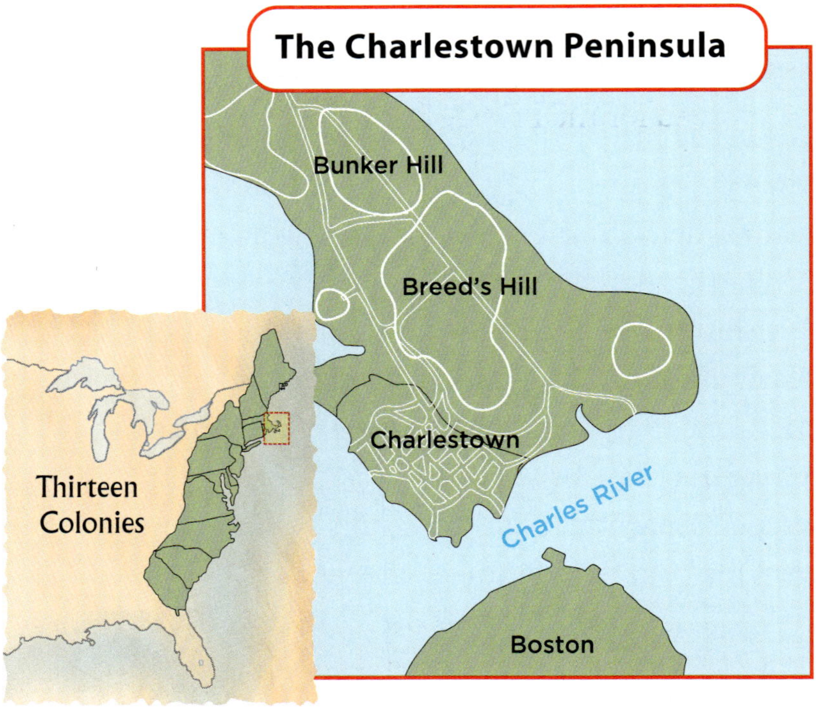

In His Own Words
John Quincy Adams

John Quincy Adams was the son of John and Abigail Adams. He grew up in Boston and later became the sixth President of the United States. He describes the experience of being under attack by the British.

"Boston became a walled town [full of] British [soldiers]. . . . For twelve months my mother with her infant children dwelt, every hour of the day and of the night with the threat of being butchered in cold blood."

The British did not think the Patriots were very smart or that they had much fighting ability. The British could not have been more wrong. Patriot spies were everywhere. They knew about British plans before some British officers found out. Patriot spies learned about British plans to take Bunker Hill. On the night of June 16, 1775, Patriot soldiers occupied Breed's Hill. They quickly built a small mud fort at the top of the hill and dug in. Then they waited for the British to arrive.

Although it is called the battle of Bunker Hill, most of the fighting took place on Breed's Hill.

★ ★ ★ Chapter Two ★ ★ ★

The Battle on the Hill

On the morning of June 17, 1775, the British woke up in Boston and could not believe their eyes. They could clearly see the Patriots on top of Breed's Hill across the river. British officers quickly got their men together. Then they set out in boats to navigate across the Charles River to Charlestown.

Who were the men on Breed's Hill? That was the question the British were asking. The Patriots were farmers and working men. Only the Patriot commanders were trained soldiers. One of them was Colonel William Prescott. He had served in the French and Indian War. Now he was the commander of a company of Patriot soldiers.

Colonel William Prescott was born in Massachusetts in 1726. ➲

Joseph Warren

Warren was a well-known doctor who counted John and Abigail Adams among his patients. A week before the Battle of Bunker Hill, he was named a major general in the Massachusetts army. Warren said he was not an experienced military man and showed up to fight at Breed's Hill as a common soldier.

Before the battle General Gage and his officers looked through a spyglass, a small telescope, at the top of Breed's Hill. "Who is that one?" asked Gage to one officer. "Will he stand and fight?"

The officer recognized Colonel Prescott. "That is Colonel Prescott—he is an old soldier, and will fight as long as a drop of blood remains in his veins."

General Israel Putnam was another soldier leading the Patriots. Putnam was full of advice for his troops. One soldier reported that Putnam said, "Powder is scarce and must not be wasted. You are all marksmen and could kill a squirrel at a hundred yards. Reserve your fire and the enemy will all be destroyed."

This illustration shows General Putnam issuing his famous order.

The Patriots Turn Back the British

By the afternoon of June 17, the British army had crossed the Charles River and landed near Breed's Hill. At 3:00 in the afternoon, the British were ready to take the hill. They marched straight up the hill in two columns stretching about a half mile across. About 2,000 British soldiers started up the hill. They marched with a swagger. In their bright red coats, they made excellent targets.

At the top of the hill 1,500 Patriot defenders waited for the enemy. They had two advantages: they were defending the higher ground, and they had plenty of spunk. But the Patriots were short of ammunition.

British Military Plans

The British did not think the colonists would stand and fight. Many British soldiers did not even have their guns loaded. They expected the colonists to run off the hill when the British got close enough to shoot.

General Israel Putnam was an experienced military leader who helped keep the Patriots together.

In his booming voice, Putnam called out to his men: "Hold your fire! Don't shoot until you can see the whites of their eyes." The British got closer and closer. Finally, at a distance of 150 yards, Putnam gave the order to fire. A huge volley of shots rang out. Many British soldiers fell dead, and the **Redcoats** retreated down the hill.

A few minutes later, the British came marching up the hill again. The Redcoats were professional soldiers. They were used to this type of battle. The Patriots admired their courage. Once more the Patriots fired into the British ranks from their place at the top of the hill. Still more Redcoats fell. The British retreated once again. The Patriots had held the hill against two British attacks. But they were just about out of ammunition.

Peter Salem's Last Shot

The British would not give up. General William Howe was the commander. Howe knew the Americans were short of ammunition. He gave orders for a third attack up the hill. He had the British troops take off their heavy packs. Without them, the British could get up the hill much faster.

For the third time that afternoon, the British soldiers marched up Breed's Hill. They stopped, fired, and then ran farther up the hill. The Patriots were out of ammunition. British soldiers swarmed into the mud fort that the Patriots had built the night before. By this time, there were about 750 Americans atop Breed's Hill. Joseph Warren was shot dead in the final attack. All seemed lost for the Patriots until Peter Salem went into action.

Major John Pitcairn

Pitcairn was a popular British officer who had been one of the commanders at the battle of Lexington. He was the commander of a company of **marines**. Pitcairn was outraged that the colonists had twice forced the British down the hill. He pushed his men to the front of the British lines. His marines were the first to reach the top.

Peter Salem was a formerly enslaved person who had been given his freedom. He had fought at the battle of Lexington and enlisted in the Patriot army. Now on Breed's Hill, Salem had saved one last shot. Major John Pitcairn was the British commander who led the assault up Breed's Hill. Pitcairn came into the fort waving his sword. Peter Salem took careful aim and fired. Pitcairn fell, badly wounded. He died a few days later.

The British soldiers were stunned to see their commander fall. They stopped fighting for a minute. In that time, the Patriot soldiers were able to get away. The British had won the hill. But they had failed to capture the Patriot defenders.

After the British soldiers retreated for the second time, officers sent more troops across the river to join the battle.

★ ★ ★ Chapter Three ★ ★ ★

Who Won?

Who won the battle of Bunker Hill? The answer seems easy. The British won the battle. They won control of Breed's and Bunker Hills. But the real answer is a little harder to understand. Let's start with how many soldiers each side lost. General Howe had about 2,400 soldiers at the battle, 1,040 of whom were killed or wounded. With a few more battles like this one, the British would have run out of soldiers. On the Patriot side 440 soldiers were lost out of about 3,200 soldiers in all.

This monument to the battle of Bunker Hill was built in 1842 and is 221 feet tall. ➲

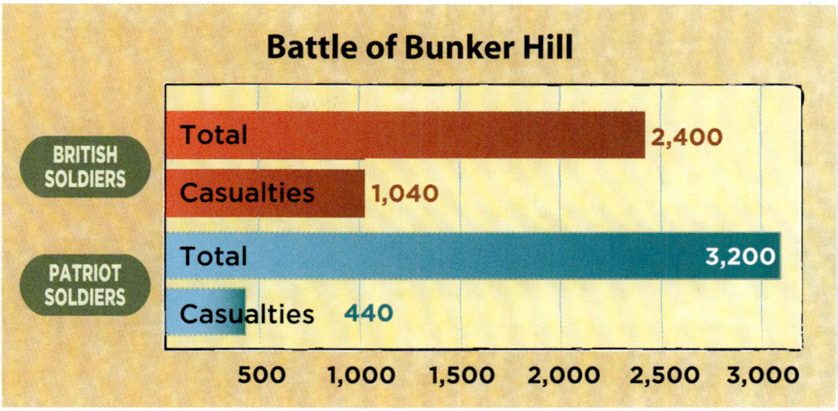

Sometimes in war the true victor of a battle cannot be seen for several years. The battle of Bunker Hill was such a battle. At the time it was considered a victory for the British. But the Patriots, who fought so bravely at Bunker Hill, proved something. They proved that they could fight the British army. The Americans had a long way to go to become a professional army. But these soldiers had been using their rifles all along to bring home dinner. They could be trained to fight together too.

The Patriots had also proven something to other Americans. In 1775 people were still making up their minds about independence. Many people thought there was no way the colonists could fight the British army. After Bunker Hill, they began to change their minds.

Abigail Adams

Abigail Adams was a remarkable woman. She had little formal education. But she read widely and listened carefully. She became one of the wisest and best-educated women in the country. She was the wife of one President, John Adams, and the mother of another, John Quincy Adams. Her husband relied on her political advice. She raised her family largely alone as her husband was often absent on political business. Later she became the first First Lady to live in the White House.

What People Saw

Most battles are only seen by the people who fight in them. But Bunker Hill was different. Many people across the river in Boston could see the battle. They climbed up to their rooftops to watch. So people from both sides told many different stories about the battle in their letters and diaries.

Abigail Adams was the wife of John Adams, a Patriot leader. Years later Adams would be elected the second President of the United States. Adams was away during the battle. Abigail told him about it in a letter.

"I have just heard that our dear friend Dr. Warren is no more but fell gloriously fighting for his country—saying better to die honorably in the field . . . . Great is our Loss."

Peter Brown was a soldier on the Patriot side. In a letter to his mother, he described the scene before the battle began:

". . . We [saw] as many as 40 boats or barges coming over, full of troops. . . . There were about 3,000 of them, and about 700 of us left."

Later Brown wrote about the end of the battle:

"Though we were but few in number, and [were] defeated by our enemy, yet we were preserved in a most wonderful manner, far beyond our expectation . . . for out of our regiment, there were but 37 killed, 4 or 5 taken captive, about 47 wounded."

Many people in Boston watched the battle of Bunker Hill.

Second Continental Congress

The violence in Massachusetts roused the colonists in all 13 colonies. It was time to take dramatic action. In May 1775, a group of Patriots met in Philadelphia. They came from all over the colonies. They were there to organize an army and to talk about forming a government. The meeting was called a **Continental Congress**. This was the second such meeting. The first one had met in 1774. The Second Continental Congress governed America from 1775 until 1788 when the U.S. Constitution was **ratified**, or approved.

The leader of the Congress was John Hancock. He had escaped capture by the British. The Congress did several important things. The most important was appointing George Washington as commander of the Continental Army. Washington was from Virginia. He had served with honor in the French and Indian War.

George Washington

George Washington's military strength lay more in his steadiness than in his brilliance. He knew the war would be a long one. As a general, Washington was careful. But when he found an opportunity to hurt the enemy, he grabbed it.

The "Olive Branch Petition" was signed by Benjamin Franklin, John Adams, Samuel Adams, Thomas Jefferson, and Patrick Henry, among others.

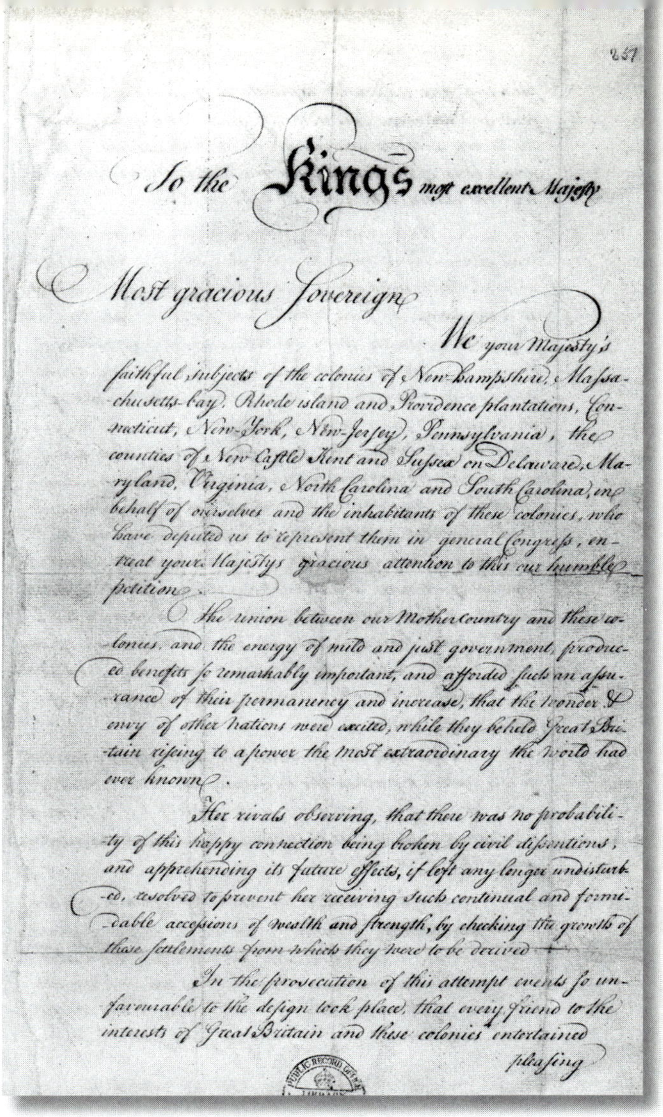

257

To the Kings most excellent Majesty

Most gracious Sovereign

We your Majesty's faithful subjects of the colonies of New-Hampshire, Massachusetts-bay, Rhode island and Providence plantations, Connecticut, New-York, New-Jersey, Pennsylvania, the counties of New Castle Kent and Sussex on Delaware, Maryland, Virginia, North Carolina and South Carolina, in behalf of ourselves and the inhabitants of these colonies, who have deputed us to represent them in general Congress, entreat your Majestys gracious attention to this our humble petition.

The union between our Mother Country and these colonies, and the energy of mild and just government, produced benefits so remarkably important, and afforded such an assurance of their permanency and increase, that the wonder & envy of other nations were excited, while they beheld Great Britain rising to a power the most extraordinary the world had ever known.

Her rivals observing, that there was no probability of this happy connection being broken by civil dissentions, and apprehending its future effects, if left any longer undisturbed, resolved to prevent her receiving such continual and formidable accessions of wealth and strength, by checking the growth of these settlements from which they were to be derived.

In the prosecution of this attempt events so unfavourable to the design took place, that every friend to the interests of Great Britain and these colonies entertained pleasing

The Congress made a last attempt to solve the crisis peacefully. It sent a **petition**, called the "Olive Branch Petition", to King George III. An olive branch is a symbol of peace. The Congress offered terms for a peaceful solution. Some British leaders supported peace. But King George was not among them. The king refused even to read the petition. He had decided to instruct the colonists in how they should behave before their king.

Conclusion ★ ★ ★

On July 2, 1775, just two weeks after the battle of Bunker Hill, George Washington arrived in Massachusetts. He took command of the Continental Army of 15,000 men. Few of them were professional soldiers. But they would fight together for more than six years. They would defeat the most powerful army in the world. How did this happen?

The road to victory started in Massachusetts. A force of soldiers, farmers, and workmen fought the British at Lexington and Concord. They fought again at Bunker Hill. The British thought they won that battle. But in it we can see the beginnings of their final defeat.

Washington's soldiers trusted his leadership.

The American Revolution

- **1769**
- **1770** Boston Massacre
- **1772**
- **1773** Boston Tea Party
- **1775** Battles of Lexington and Concord
- **1776** Declaration of Independence signed

George Washington studied the battle of Bunker Hill. From it he learned an important lesson. Winning battles was certainly better than losing them. But the most important thing on the Americans' side was time. The Americans needed to keep the war going. The longer the war went on, the more likely the British would get tired of fighting it. Washington also knew that the longer the war went on, the more likely it was that the British would make a mistake.

Washington was right. The war went on for six years. The British did make several big mistakes that allowed the Americans to win. The British government got tired of fighting and finally agreed to American independence.

How did a ragtag group of Americans defeat the most powerful army in the world? British soldiers fought because it was their job. The Patriots won because they were fighting for their freedom. They believed in their cause. And so, the thirteen British colonies became the United States of America.

1777
Battle of Saratoga—Americans win great victory

1778
France enters the war on the side of the United States

1781
Battle of Yorktown—British surrender

1783
Treaty of Paris ends the war; Great Britain recognizes American independence

1778 — 1781 — 1784

Glossary

Continental Congress *(KON-tuh-nen-tuhl KONG-gris)* Patriot governing body that formed the American army and set up a government *(page 18)*

marine *(muh-REEN)* a soldier trained to fight on land and water *(page 13)*

massacre *(MAS-uh-kur)* the brutal killing of a group of people *(page 3)*

militia *(muh-LISH-uh)* an army of citizens who are not professional soldiers *(page 4)*

Minutemen *(MIN-it-men)* Patriot militia trained to respond "at a minute's warning" *(page 4)*

Patriot *(PAY-tree-uht)* an American colonist who favored independence *(page 3)*

petition *(puh-TISH-uhn)* a formal request made to the person in charge. A petition usually contains a statement and the signatures of people who support it. *(page 19)*

ratify *(RAT-uh-figh)* to approve officially *(page 18)*

rebellion *(ri-BEL-yuhn)* an armed uprising against one's government *(page 3)*

Redcoat *(RED-koht)* the name Patriots used to describe British soldiers, who wore bright red coats as part of their uniform *(page 11)*

tyrant *(TIGH-ruhnt)* someone who rules other people in a cruel or unjust way *(page 3)*

Index

Adams, Abigail, *7, 9, 16*

Adams, John, *7, 9, 16, 19*

Adams, John Quincy, *7, 16*

Adams, Samuel, *3–5, 19*

battle of Bunker Hill, *6–17, 20–21*

battle of Concord, *4–5, 20*

battle of Lexington, *4–5, 13, 20*

Boston Massacre, *3, 20*

Boston Tea Party, *3, 20*

Breed's Hill, *6–10, 12–14*

Brown, Peter, *17*

Constitution, *18*

Gage, Governor Thomas, *4, 9*

George III, King, *3, 19*

Hancock, John, *4–5, 18*

Howe, General William, *12, 14*

Intolerable Acts, *4*

marines, *13*

Minutemen, *4–6*

"Olive Branch Petition", *19*

Pitcairn, Major John, *13*

Prescott, Colonel William, *8–9*

Putnam, General Israel, *9–11*

Redcoats, *11*

Revere, Paul, *5*

Salem, Peter, *12–13*

Second Continental Congress, *18–19*

thirteen colonies, *2, 18, 21*

Warren, Dr. Joseph, *9, 12, 16*

Washington, General George, *18, 20–21*

Comprehension Check

Summarize

Use a Conclusion Chart to help you retell *The Battle of Bunker Hill*. Tell what happened at the Battle of Bunker Hill by listing clues in the text for each conclusion you draw.

Text Clues	Conclusion

Think and Compare

1. Turn to page 10. What advantages and disadvantages did the Patriots have in the battle of Bunker Hill? ***(Draw Conclusions)***
2. Why do you think that General Putnam had the Americans hold their fire until the British were close to the top of Breed's Hill? ***(Analyze)***
3. The Patriot soldiers at Bunker Hill were fighting for their freedom. What does freedom mean to you? What freedoms do you appreciate? ***(Evaluate)***